On My Own at 107

Reflections on Life Without Bessie

Sarah L. Delany
with
Amy Hill Hearth

Illustrations by Brian M. Kotzky

HarperSanFrancisco
An Imprint of HarperCollins*Publishers*

Opposite page: Bessie Delany in New York City, around 1933. Photograph courtesy of the authors.

ON MY OWN AT 107: *Reflections on Life Without Bessie.* Copyright © 1997 by Sarah L. Delany and Amy Hill Hearth. All rights reserved. Printed in the United States of America. No part of this book may be used or reproduced in any manner whatsoever without written permission except in the case of brief quotations embodied in critical articles and reviews. For information address HarperCollins Publishers, 10 East 53RD Street, New York, NY 10022.

HarperCollins Web Site: http://www.harpercollins.com
HarperCollins®, ☕ ®, and HarperSanFrancisco™ are trademarks of HarperCollins Publishers Inc.

FIRST EDITION

Library of Congress Cataloging-in-Publication Data
Delany, Sarah Louise
On my own at 107 : reflections on life without Bessie / Sarah L. Delany with Amy Hill Hearth.
ISBN 0–06–251485–7 (cloth)   ISBN 0–06–251486–5 (pbk.)
1. Afro-Americans–Biography. 2. Delany family. 3. Delany, Sarah Louise. 4. Delany, Annie Elizabeth.
E185.96.D375 1997   920'.009296073–DC21   96-45282

99 00 01 ❖ RRDH 10 9 8 7 6 5 4 3

Dedicated with love and affection and in memory
of Dr. Annie Elizabeth Delany
"Our Bessie"

Contents

The authors would like to thank Blair A. Hearth, husband
of Amy Hill Hearth; our literary agent, Daniel A. Strone,
Vice President of the William Morris Agency;
Logan D. Delany, Jr., grandnephew of the Delany sisters;
and our editor at HarperSanFrancisco,
Caroline Pincus, for their support
in creating this book.

Special thanks to J. Benjamin Williams & Associates of
Silver Spring, Maryland, for creating the magnificent Delany
Sisters Rose and presenting it to Sadie Delany on her 107TH
birthday. Additionally, a heartfelt thank-you is owed Debra
Bard of the William Morris Agency and the staff of
HarperSanFrancisco for their hard work in making
the Delany Sisters Rose a reality.

Finally, thanks to Brian M. Kotzky of Glen Cove,
New York, for capturing the essence and spirit
of Bessie Delany in his watercolor illustrations
of the flowers from her
beloved garden.

∽o∾

On September 25, 1995, Dr. Annie Elizabeth ("Bessie") Delany died at home in Mount Vernon, New York, at the age of 104, marking the end not only of an extraordinary life but a century-long relationship with her beloved older sister, Sarah, known as Sadie.

Bessie and Sadie Delany found fame and received accolades at the ages of 102 and 104 as coauthors, along with myself, of *Having Our Say: The Delany Sisters' First 100 Years,* published in 1993. The memoir, which stayed on the *New York Times* bestseller list for more than two years, was adapted to the stage and became a Broadway hit (also called *Having Our Say*) in the spring of 1995. The sisters and I published a critically acclaimed sequel, *The Delany Sisters' Book of Everyday Wisdom,* in 1994.

I first met the Delany sisters in 1991 as a journalist on assignment for the *New York Times.* When I knocked on their door, hoping for an

interesting interview, I could never have antici-
pated the treasure that awaited me. My article led
to *Having Our Say,* a collaboration that took two
years to complete.

Millions of people around the world are now
acquainted with the delightful and charming
Delany sisters, and *Having Our Say* has been
added to the history curriculum at countless
schools and colleges.

Long before being "discovered" (a term Bessie
often used with great delight) at the ages of 100
and 102, the sisters had led fascinating lives. They
were members of a prominent family that was
well known among a small but elite circle within
the black community in the 1920s and 1930s. The
sisters enjoyed a certain status, but it was the six
Delany brothers—particularly the handsome and
charismatic Hubert Delany, a New York City
judge who ran unsuccessfully for Congress—who
garnered most of the attention in the black press.

Born on the campus of Saint Augustine's
School (now College) in Raleigh, North Carolina,
the ten Delany siblings were the children of
Henry Beard Delany, a man born into slavery who
eventually became the first elected black

Episcopal bishop in the United States. Their mother, Nanny Logan Delany, was born free to a white man and his beloved lifelong partner, a woman of color. Nanny Logan Delany, who could have "passed" for white, proudly chose to live as a black woman instead.

The Delany sisters graduated from Saint Augustine's and worked as teachers in the South to save money to further their education. Later, they joined the historic migration of black Americans who headed north in search of opportunity, arriving in New York City during World War I.

In 1923, Bessie Delany graduated from Columbia University's School of Dental and Oral Surgery. She was only the second black woman licensed to practice dentistry in New York. For many years she ran a thriving dental practice in Harlem and was known as "Dr. Bessie" to her patients and throughout the black community.

Sadie, meanwhile, attended Pratt Institute and later Columbia University in pursuit of a teaching degree. She earned her bachelor's degree in 1920 at Columbia and a master's, also at Columbia, in 1925. Sadie was the first black woman to teach domestic science on the high-school level in New York City.

The Delany sisters lived in Harlem during the era known as the Harlem Renaissance and mingled with writers such as Langston Hughes and jazz musicians including Duke Ellington and Cab Calloway. Bessie Delany was an activist for women's and civil rights, naming among her friends Dr. W. E. B. Du Bois and James Weldon Johnson.

Neither Bessie nor Sadie was interested in marriage, although they had many suitors. As the sisters explained it, they would have been expected to give up their careers had they married. This was an option the independent-minded Delany sisters were not willing to consider.

For companionship, the two sisters lived together, an arrangement they continued throughout their lives. After living in Harlem for many years, the sisters moved to a cottage in the Bronx and finally, in 1957, to a two-story house in Mount Vernon, New York, where Sadie continues to live today.

The Delany sisters were devoted to each other, but they were not alike. Indeed, they could not have been more different in personality. Sadie, the elder sister, is gentle and calm. Bessie, the "little" sister, was feisty and outspoken. The two sisters accepted, respected, and even poked fun at their differences.

Inevitably, this remarkable, century-long relationship came to a close with the death of one of the sisters. Perhaps surprisingly, it was the younger sister, Bessie, who died first. In the year preceding her death, Bessie had become increasingly frail. Those of us who loved her could see that she was fading away before our eyes. She died as she had wanted: at home, in her bed, with Sadie nearby.

True to form, Bessie managed to "have her say" at her own funeral! A few months before her death, she took my hand and said, "Amy, when the time comes, tell 'em the old gal was quite happy." She made it very clear that she wanted me to speak those words to comfort her mourners at her funeral. Three days after her death, at the Cathedral of Saint John the Divine in New York City, I stood up and repeated her words. As my words echoed in the huge cathedral, I looked past the throng of mourners, the celebrities in the front row, and the television cameras and newspaper photographers recording the event. I saw only Sadie, dressed in a brown suit with a matching beret, crumpling and uncrumpling a handkerchief in her lap in some unconscious ritual of grief.

At first, the loss of Bessie seemed unbearable. At the time, Sadie Delany had just turned 106 and was on her own for the first time in her life. Always known as one-half of a pair, her identity forged since birth as one of the Delany sisters, Sadie suddenly found herself, unwillingly, an individual.

One of her first reactions, however, revealed her resilience. When an interviewer asked her what she would do now, after the death of her sister, she said, "Another book!" Then she turned to me and said, "If that's okay with you, Amy." I laughed and said, "Of course," delighted at this powerful indication that Sadie had hope for the future. Indeed, creating this book would give new meaning to Sadie's life, providing a mechanism for her to express her feelings as well as fulfilling her ongoing need to be useful and productive.

On My Own at 107: Reflections on Life Without Bessie is Sadie's tribute to her little sister. It is also a memoir of Sadie's first year after Bessie's death—the story of one woman's evolution, over the course of a year, from despair to hope. Sadie Delany has given us an invaluable gift: she shows us that even at the age of 107 it is possible to begin again.

—*Amy Hill Hearth*

Part One

*T*he winter began early that year with a fierce snowstorm in early November, six weeks after Bessie died. Sadie watched from the window as the falling snow quickly covered Bessie's beloved flower garden. She had been caught unprepared. Some of the shrubs had not yet been covered for winter.

The snowstorm would be the first of many that season. Each time it snowed, Sadie held her vigil by the window. Passersby could sometimes see her sitting motionless, staring out, as if waiting for someone to come up the walk. It was a time of long silences.

An unusual winter, they said. The worst in New York since 1946; no, the worst ever recorded. The heavy snowfalls disrupted lives and schedules. Everything else was secondary to the weather.

For Sadie, the relentless snowstorms increased her isolation. Unable to venture out, afraid of falling or catching cold, she remained indoors, dependent on the young and hardy to visit her. It was as if some force were keeping her there, indoors by the window, contemplating her enormous loss.

Not necessarily a bad thing, she thought one day. It gave her time alone to think. To herself, and to the few who visited, she spoke quietly of Bessie. Often she even spoke *to* Bessie. Graveyard talk, she called it. The kind of things you say to a tombstone when you visit a cemetery and no one can overhear.

Then one day in early spring, just when it seemed winter might never end, Sadie ventured outdoors and was greeted by a wondrous sight: Bessie's crocus plants were peeking through the snow.

It was a moment that Bessie had celebrated every year. Sadie remembered how Bessie would come rushing inside, all excited, saying, "Sadie, Sadie, my crocus plants are here!" They would rejoice, for it meant that springtime and all it signifies was on its way at last.

Soon the other plants would be blooming, too, Sadie knew. It gave her courage.

Planted in the house of Yahweh,
they will flourish in the courts of our God,
still bearing fruit in old age,
still remaining fresh and green . . .

PSALM 92:13–14, JB

One

I SURE MISS YOU, OLD GAL.

The Lord left me here, and took you. He took my little sister. More than 104 years by my side, and now you're gone.

I just keep telling myself, you're up there with Mama and Papa, and all our brothers and sisters. You've gone to Glory. You're in a better place.

I have to tell you the truth. This being alone is *hard*. For the first time in my life, I don't have you by my side. I'm 107 years old now and it's like I'm just learning how to walk.

I still get up early in the morning and say my prayers, just as we always did. I do my yoga exercises. I eat my breakfast. I read my mail. But you're not there to do these things with me.

Letting go of you was the hardest thing I've ever done. The day of the funeral was the longest day of my life. I made sure the funeral was done right. I wanted to be sure my sister had a proper send-off! We had a big funeral, with all the dignitaries, at the Cathedral of Saint John the Divine in New York City. Oh, it was a big affair. You'd have been tickled by it.

Bessie, I wanted to walk into that old church myself, up those steps and down that long aisle, but they wouldn't let me. I went in a wheelchair, so I wouldn't get tired.

Two things stand out in my mind from that day. One was a group of schoolchildren from Harlem. They were kind of shy, but they came up to me at the church with these beautiful handmade cards. You would have liked that. The other thing I re-member was that the bishop permitted me, as a special honor, to sprinkle holy water on the casket. I tried all day to be strong but that's when I broke down crying.

I asked our nephew Lemuel Jr. to handle every-thing, since he's an undertaker. After the service, he drove straight down to North Carolina in the hearse. He took you home. Left New York City and drove straight on down there. I knew you were in good hands, little sister.

Now you may think this is crazy, but I went down to Raleigh for the burial. I flew down there in an airplane, yes indeed! I had to see it for myself. I had to see my sister buried.

We had another service in Raleigh. This was the first time I'd been back to the campus of Saint Augustine's since you and I went to visit about twenty years ago. Oh, Bessie, things have changed. Most of the old buildings are gone. But the chapel's still standing that Papa built with his own hands, a hundred years ago.

I did everything just as we had planned. I left that space for me in the family plot between you and Mama, just like you wanted. I remember how you used to say that I should have the space next to Mama since I was the Mama's child. I always thought that was awful sweet of you.

When you live this long, you sure bury a lot of people. Now I feel like I've outlived everybody! Mama and Papa are long gone; all of our brothers and sisters are gone. I'm the only one left.

I'm trying real hard not to indulge in self-pity. It just makes me feel worse if I do. Only one time since you left us, dear little sister, did I allow myself to feel sorry for myself. It was about two weeks after you left us. I felt despair that you were gone and frustrated because I can't do everything I want anymore. *What good am I?* I thought.

One of our young friends stopped by while I was feeling like that and I told her what I'd been thinking.

"Well, *I* need you," she said. "Don't you go leaving me." And we laughed.

Afterwards, I felt ashamed. I kind of laughed at myself. Why, I have been so blessed in my life!

Crocus

*"Bessie so admired the brave little crocus plants,
pushing their way through the frozen earth.
The purple ones are known
as 'Remembrance.'"*

∽o∾

Two

A FEW DAYS AFTER YOU LEFT US, BESSIE, I started wearing one of your suitcoats—you know, the gray one you loved so much. It made me feel good, having it wrapped around me.

I have so much mail to answer, I keep busy. Folks from all over the world are sending condolence cards. I think it is mighty sweet, and I try to answer every one, but I've about worn myself out.

My mind keeps going back to this idea that maybe if I'd taken better care of you, you'd still be here. I keep thinking, *Maybe I should have done things differently. Maybe I should have had someone get a doctor or ambulance.* Oh, I don't know. Sometimes it's harder to be the one left behind than the one doing the dyin'.

I've had to break a century of habits, letting go of you, old gal. Just little things, like expecting you to be there to set the table. All of a sudden there is no one to check the furnace when it acts up. No one to give me a hard time about this and that!

I never was a big cryer. But I think that sometimes there's not a thing you can do but just cry. I just keep telling myself over and over, *To be absent from the body means to be present with the Lord.*

About two weeks after you left us, I came down with a terrible cold. Now you know I am never sick. Everyone was just convinced I would get pneumonia and die.

I guess I could have died very easily. I suppose I could have just given up, succumbed to it. But I fought it. I'm not sure why. Much as I want to join you in Glory, I knew it wasn't my time yet.

All our homefolks convinced me that I should not be living alone anymore. So we asked Dawn, that Jamaican gal who is such a good cook, to start spending more time with me. She's like a companion, in case I fall or need help or something like that. Funny thing is, she's feisty as can be—just like you!

One thing I've learned, Bessie, is that things change whether you like it or not. I sure didn't want you to go, but you had to.

We all wish that things could stay the same, but they won't. We all wish we could live forever, but we can't. I wonder what it is about life that makes us cling to it so, especially since the world can be so cruel sometimes.

As the Lord said, it's not up to us to understand everything. Sooner or later, we all have to go to the Spirit World. Some folks live 10 years and some 110, and only the Lord knows why.

Tulip

"Bessie liked to add new plants to her garden every year. After she died, someone gave me some tulip bulbs to add to the garden. I planted them and it made me happy. I know that they'll be back next year."

Three

I GOT A LETTER THE OTHER DAY ADDRESSED TO "The Delany Sisters." And it hit me that there really isn't any such thing anymore. There's only me. There's only Sadie. No more "Sadie and Bessie." No more "Delany sisters."

Now that about breaks my heart. I've been your other half for more than a hundred years. It's like a married couple. You kind of merge into one person after a while.

Just like a widow who thinks of herself as somebody's wife, I think of myself as Bessie Delany's sister.

Since you left us just a few weeks after your birthday I was still receiving birthday cards for you after you were gone! And at the same time I started to get condolence cards. I don't think anything upset me more than to see condolence cards mixed in with birthday cards. I kept thinking, *Poor Bessie never got to see these lovely birthday cards.*

Then I started feeling bad for the people who sent the birthday cards. I thought, *I bet they mailed them before they heard that Bessie died, and now they feel terrible.*

I'm *still* receiving mail for you, Bessie, and it always makes me feel a little bad. Someone told me that it's because folks use these computers today and your name is on a list and the stupid computers don't know that you died. So I still keep getting mail in your name.

The worst was when we received an invitation to attend an event in our honor—and the invitation arrived a month after you died! One invitation was addressed to me, and one to you. I was just furious. I think the folks who own these computers should be more considerate.

I never thought I could live without you, but here I am, like it or not. When you left us, I guess everybody expected me to up and die, too. Remember how I used to say, "I wouldn't last two weeks without Bessie."

The unthinkable happened. I felt like someone had cut off one of my arms. Somebody said, "There's probably nobody on Earth who has lived together for so long!" And I'm thinking that may well be true. So I'm charting new ground, Bessie.

I'm very conscious of being alone. I notice your absence in everything I do. When I do my exercises, I still have this urge to look over at you to see if you're doing them right. Sometimes it makes me laugh because I remember how you used to cheat!

You'd think we were Siamese twins who couldn't live without each other! Well, I'm learning that I am a separate human being. For the first time in my life, I'm learning that.

Here I am, the older sister of the pair; it doesn't seem natural that I've outlived you. I guess God wasn't ready to take me home yet. There's a proper order to things but only He knows what it is.

I heard of a little girl who was upset when she heard one of the Delany sisters died, and perplexed that the younger one had died first. It didn't make sense to her.

I'm pretty sure that you thought we'd both go at about the same time. We didn't plan on one of us surviving the other for very long. Maybe it was too terrible to think about.

I remember something you used to say. "Don't waste a single day; it's not yours to waste." Oh, how right you were. What arrogance human beings have to act like life goes on forever! We sit and fuss over silly things, yet once the moment's passed it's gone. We know it in our brains but we don't act upon this knowledge.

Just this morning I told a young friend of ours that she had better start spending more time with her parents. I told her, "You act like your parents are going to live forever. I'm sorry to tell you, but they won't. Enjoy them now."

I get upset now when folks put things off for a "rainy day." Well, that rainy day might never come. I had a young visitor the other day who was talking about going back to college. I said, "Stop talking about it—do it now! The world is not going to wait for you."

Daylily

"Bessie always grew daylilies
wherever we lived, even in the Bronx,
back in the '40s. Mama was still alive then,
and I remember her helping Bessie
plant them in the garden there.
Bessie got her love of gardening
from Mama."

∽ o ∽

Four

THE WINTER AFTER YOU LEFT US WAS THE longest, coldest, snowiest one that anyone had ever seen in these parts. It seemed fitting, somehow. It makes you feel small. It reminds you, *So many things are out of our hands.*

But once the spring came I began to feel better. How can you not feel optimistic when the days are longer and warmer? And the birds are singing? The spring reminded me, *Life goes on.*

Bessie, I think you loved your garden as much as you loved me! You took care of every shrub and every flower. And now, when I go out there, I feel your presence.

Now I'm not saying that I've seen apparitions or anything like that. But I can feel your spirit, especially in that garden.

Dawn, that Jamaican gal who has been keeping me company, used to sleep in your bed right after you left us but said she can't sleep there no more. Says she woke up one night and there you were, just standing over her, looking at her. Poor thing about died. Bessie, you should know better than to go around scaring folks like that.

I've been dreaming about you, just about every time I close my eyes. One time I dreamed you were still living. A man came up the walk and I said to you, "Why, that man looks just like Papa," and you said, "It *is* Papa." And Mama was there, too, and she jumped up and ran to greet him.

I don't know what it all means. Maybe it doesn't mean anything, maybe it does. I guess, at the least, it means that all my people who have gone to Glory are alive in my heart and mind. They're still with me, and as long as I'm living they'll be a part of my life.

I surely hope I get to see you all again one day. I believe in the Father, the Son, and the Holy Ghost. I hope Heaven is what I expect it will be. It's hard to picture, but I think it'll be very beautiful and probably different than anything we could imagine down here on Earth. I want to be reunited with my mama and my sister and all my home-folks. If not, I surely will be disappointed!

A friend of ours said, "Just think of learning to live without Bessie as a challenge. You've faced challenges all your life; this is a new one."

Now that got me thinking. It's true that I never ran from a challenge. Why, I fought prejudice because of the color of my skin! I fought prejudice as a woman! I've fought prejudice as an older person! (You know how it is—when you get past one hundred, folks just assume you don't have any sense!)

I wasn't as direct about my battles as you were, Bessie, but I was pretty relentless and determined in my own way, yes indeed. Remember how I got my promotion to teach at a white high school? I wanted that job because it paid better and was a step up, but they wouldn't hire me because I was colored. So I ignored that letter inviting me for an interview, where they would have seen that I was colored. I played dumb. I pretended there was a mix-up in the mail and just showed up on the first day of classes. They were mad as wet hens, but they were stuck with me.

It seems peculiar in a way, looking at being alone as a challenge. But it helps. I thought, *A difficult road to travel, but not impassable.*

We were brought up to rise to the occasion. Remember how Papa used to say, "Reach high! Reach high!"

I'll tell you something else that helps. That old saying "Take life one day at a time" is mighty good advice. If I find myself becoming overwhelmed by it all, I focus on getting through the rest of the day, or maybe just through dinner, or just through the next hour without you.

Sometimes all this sadness, well, it kind of makes me angry. I get fed up with it. I don't like being sad. I'm not a sad person, really. I wasn't meant to be sad all the time.

Once in a while I can't help but think that if you had tried harder, if you had really wanted to, you would have kept going. You wouldn't have left me here alone.

I guess I'm no different from any human being: we're all a little greedy. I just wanted more time with you, just the way things were. Another day, another week, another year. It's really selfish, I know. I guess it's human nature. At times we all think the sun rises and sets over our house and no one else's.

Someone said, "Bessie was 104 years old. She couldn't live forever!" And I realized, of course, that is so.

Poppy

"Oh, how Bessie loved poppies,
especially the red ones. She sprinkled them
throughout the garden—bright splashes
of color on the landscape."

⌘

Part Two

*S*pring was more glorious that year than any Sadie could remember. Did it only seem that way because the winter had been so long and hard? Or was it simply that all the snow had melted and nourished the soil?

As more flowers began to bloom in Bessie's garden, Sadie felt hopeful. Almost a sense of excitement, she thought, or perhaps relief. At least something was right with the world.

Sometimes it seemed odd that the flowers would return at all. How could they, with Bessie gone? But the tender plants responded to the sun and the rain. Oblivious to the passing of the mistress who tended and cultivated them, the flowers reached for the sun.

Like little sentries outside Sadie's window, the flowers guarded Bessie's memory. Each little patch that popped up as spring turned into summer was a reminder that Bessie had been a presence on this earth. It was she who planted and nurtured the flowers through spring rain and summer drought, their hardiness a testament to her devotion.

What pleasant memories Sadie had of Bessie outdoors, gloved and hatted, crouched peering at some needy plant. Her hands, the hands of a dentist—strong and supple—were often her only tools. She knew she should wear gloves but often didn't, preferring the feel of the earth on her skin. Her hands, oversized for a woman and always a source of a little embarrassment, were not an encumbrance in the garden.

Bessie had found happiness in the garden. Sadie remembered how her sister talked to the plants as if they were human. "Oh, you little darlings," she'd say to the pansies. Or, "Aren't you gorgeous?" to her roses.

Many of Bessie's characteristics became apparent in the garden. She was affectionate and tender. She was devoted and determined. She was sometimes stubborn.

Sadie remembered how Bessie would get mad at the wild ficus trees that would grow so quickly they'd block the distant view of New York City from the porch in a matter of days. This annoyed

Bessie. She'd climb a ladder and cut them down, scolding them as if they were naughty children. She did this until she was ninety-eight years old.

Sometimes Sadie would join Bessie in the garden. At other times, she would watch Bessie from the window. There she'd be, on bended knee, or squatting for hours on end. Sometimes she'd disappear momentarily from view, returning with a hoe or watering can.

It was not hard to imagine her out there still.

. . . in the morning it flourishes and is renewed;
in the evening it fades and withers.

The days of our life are seventy years,
or perhaps eighty, if we are strong;
even then their span is only toil and trouble;
they are soon gone, and we fly away.

PSALM 90:6, 10, NRSV

Five

SOMEONE ASKED ME WHEN I MISS YOU MOST. Well, I'd say that's at night. Sometimes I wake in the middle of the night calling your name.

Every evening now, I watch the day turn to night. The streetlights come on. The birds rush to and fro and then finally settle down.

Bessie, that mean old black squirrel is still hanging around. He runs around on the phone wires and on the big sycamore tree, bossing around all the other squirrels.

There's a stray cat now, a big yellow tomcat. At first I thought it was our big old cat, Mr. Delany. I remember how you and I nursed that old cat back to health after we found him in the street that day. Ungrateful rascal went and ran out on us! You used to say he must be dead, because otherwise he would have come back.

All the children in the neighborhood are getting so big I hardly know them and I suppose you wouldn't either. Remember that little white child who got stuck in the fence that day and you got him out? Well, I figure it's been twenty years since that happened.

I remember when we heard that boy died a few years ago; took his own life as a young man. And you cried and cried and fretted for days. "If only I had known there was a problem, maybe I could have done something," you kept saying. I always said you felt things deeply, Bessie. A lot of folks never understood how you suffered for it.

You were sensitive from the day you were born until the day you died. I was never as sensitive, and I wonder now if my life was easier because of it. I walked down "the sunny side of the street," as they used to say.

And you? You used to say about yourself, "It ain't easy being Bessie." I used to find it amusing but now I understand what you meant.

Rhododendron

*"There was an old ladies' home
in our neighborhood, and for years the
women would come by and admire Bessie's garden.
I remember one lady was crazy about Bessie's
rhododendrons. We used to invite
her to sit and enjoy the garden."*

✌︎

Six

I REMEMBER YOU SAYING ONCE, A FEW YEARS ago, "Sadie, do you suppose we're ever going to die?" It did seem rather peculiar, both of us living past one hundred, outliving everybody around us. We wondered, *What does the Lord have in store for us? Why is this happening?*

Year after year, we kept celebrating those birthdays. Every year you'd say, "Well, maybe this is the last one."

You were a part of my life since I was two years old. I don't remember life without you. I can see your face in every memory from my own childhood: playing with our dolls, picking cotton to make a little money, learning how to ride Papa's horse, making candy outdoors at Eastertime. Yes, you were always there.

And now you're gone.

We talked a lot about death and dying over the years. For a while there, once you got past one hundred, you drove me a little crazy talking about it. I think you had in mind this big Hollywood death scene with certain people at your bedside. And one day I finally said, "Bessie, you know that's not real life. I don't think you can choreograph it, for Heaven's sake."

Then you started talking about dying in your sleep. You told everybody, "I've decided I want to die in my sleep. I think that'll be good."

I was kind of annoyed at that. I said, "Good for you, maybe, but not necessarily for me! I'm the one that will have to find you dead in your bed!"

Then you changed your mind *again*.

"I don't want to die in my sleep," you declared.

And I said, "Why?" (I'm sure I sounded quite exasperated.)

"Well, if I die in my sleep I might miss something!"

And I said, "Oh, Bessie, enough already!"

I never saw anyone who felt things more deeply than you did. When you were mad, you were furious. When you were happy, you were full of joy.

You grieved about things that most people would shrug off. Remember when we hired that fella to help you in the garden? And he didn't listen to your instructions and he cut down the little plum tree we took from our grandfather's farm?

You came into the house and I knew something terrible had happened. One look at your face and I said, "Lord, did someone die?"

And you said, "Not someone, but some*thing*." You told me what happened and I was upset. But you—you held your head in your hands. I think you missed that little plum tree 'til the day you died.

Once something—or someone—was in your care you never let go. That reminds me of Amelia. When I was down in Raleigh everybody was asking me who "Amelia" was in the family plot. Seems none of them knew the story of your little friend Amelia.

"Amelia was Bessie's classmate at Saint Augustine's," I said. "She came to New York about the same time we did, during World War I. Later on—must've been during the '40s and '50s—Amelia was hospitalized on Staten Island. She was institutionalized for many years, destitute and bedridden from diabetes."

And I told them how you said to me, "Sadie, we can't abandon poor Amelia." So every Saturday, for years, we traveled to Staten Island from our cottage in the Bronx to see her.

We were the only people who visited Amelia for many years. When Amelia died, she disowned her family and left two thousand dollars to us—all the money she had in the world. She had asked that we bury her in Raleigh if possible, but not with her people.

And you said, "Sadie, let's take Amelia down to Raleigh and put her with Mama and Papa. I think she would have liked that." So you took the two thousand dollars and spent it sending the body down there and having a proper burial.

That's what makes me so sure you got into Heaven. I'm sure folks like Amelia were up there putting in a good word for you!

Coral Bells

*"Bessie loved coral bells
because they were so dainty. The ones
she planted in her garden she took from
our little sister Julia's flowerbeds in the
Bronx almost forty years ago."*

❧⭒❦

Seven

I KNEW YOU WERE LEAVING US WHEN YOU WEREN'T up to working in your garden anymore. That summer was so long and hot and dry. No rain fell for weeks on end. The flowers in the garden barely grew. Looking back on it now, I wonder if it was an omen of things to come.

I tried to hire a gardener, but I couldn't get anyone to do it as nice as you did. And I know it made you feel bad—the idea of someone messing with your garden. But I wanted it to look good 'cause I thought it would cheer you up. I guess in some way I thought that it would make you strong again, make you want to live.

The first thing I did when it sunk into my head that you had left us, Bessie, was to pray. I think I could feel your spirit fly to the sky. I prayed that you were on your way to the Lord and that you would be accepted into His arms.

I said, "Lord, please take Bessie into your care. She is a sweet, sweet child." I pleaded with the Lord to let you into Heaven. I said, "Please forgive her for being mean sometimes. She really is a good person!"

I'm still praying for you. I've put your name at the top of my prayer list ahead of Mama and Papa and everyone else.

I say, "Dear Lord, Please bless and keep Bessie, Mr. Miliam and Grandma, Mama and Papa, Lemuel, Julia, Hap, Manross, Lucius, Hubert, Laura, and Sam. . . ."

The list, as you well know, goes on and on. I try not to neglect anyone. I think I've got everybody covered. Grandparents, parents, brothers and sisters, and so on. Folks are always asking me to add them to my prayer list and of course I always say yes. How could I say no?

I remember your last days when you were too tired to list everyone by name. You used to say, "And, Lord, bless and keep *all* of my loved ones."

That was kind of a shortcut. I know you felt a little guilty because you thought that was cheating a bit, but mercy, who could blame you?

Well, I'm still trying to list each and every person. Otherwise I would have a very guilty conscience and at this point in my life that is something I do not want to have. Anything that increases my chances of getting into Heaven I'm willing to do. I have said my prayers every day for 107 years and I'm not about to skip a day now. The way I see it, it would be a shame if I skipped a day and then *that* was the day the Lord called me home. So I'm praying and praying and praying.

I remember when we were little how Mama always had her hour of prayer every afternoon. No matter what was happening, everything stopped. She'd go into her room and sit at her writing desk and read the Bible and pray. Mama was the busiest woman alive—running the day-to-day operations at Saint Aug's, being married to a priest, and having ten children. But she always made time for prayer.

Prayer is a comfort that keeps you going in good times and bad. During good times, it's a way of saying thanks and acknowledging your blessings.

In bad times, it's something to lean on during your hour of trial.

There's comfort in the words. I can still hear Papa's voice as he prayed in church and at home. And Mama's voice, too. And yours. We prayed together as a family.

I remember Papa's prayer at mealtimes: "Bless, we beseech Thee, O Lord, this food which we are about to partake. May it strengthen us to do our service. For Christ's sake, Amen."

Mama's prayer at mealtime was, "Bless, O Lord, the food before us, for Christ's sake, Amen." You see, Mama's prayer was shorter. Well, she was the mother of ten children. She was in a hurry, you know.

Now I am praying alone, at mealtime and before bed. I still keep my prayer book on the nightstand with my favorite picture of Mama inside to mark the place. Maybe I should put a picture of you there, too, Bessie.

Iris

*"Bessie aimed to have flowers
blooming in an overlapping fashion,
so that there was never a day when something
was not at its most radiant. The irises
usually made their appearance
in May."*

✎⊙✎

Eight

FOLKS ASK ME WHY I'VE LIVED SUCH A LONG AND happy life and I always say the Lord deserves the credit. Another factor, I'm sure, is that it runs in the family. Why, Mama lived to be ninety-five years old with no medical intervention whatsoever.

Another reason is the way we live—exercise, eating lots of fruits and vegetables, no smoking, things like that. Plenty of folks want to know what makes us tick, don't they, Bessie? I remember how doctors suggested that we leave our bodies to science so they could try to figure us out, but you were absolutely opposed to it, ever since that one doctor tracked us down a few years back.

The doctor got right to the point. She said she was in charge of some kind of "brain project" and wanted our brains after we died!

I guess it was the way she asked that annoyed you so much, Bessie. You said, "Honey, you're crazy. You say you want my brain? I've got news for you. I came into the world with it. And I'll be taking it with me when I go!"

Now, I think a lot of credit for our longevity should go to Mama and Papa for the way they raised us. We didn't have any money as a family, growing up, but we lived a godly life. And we learned good habits, how to take care of ourselves properly. We ate well because there was a farm on the campus of Saint Aug's.

What we didn't have at Saint Aug's, Papa would get for us one way or another. I remember Papa going off to the market in Raleigh at the end of the day and buying wagonloads of fruit that hadn't sold that day. The farmers were anxious to get rid of it, so Papa bought it cheap. A whole wagonload of watermelons, for a *dime*.

To think that we used to share one scrawny little chicken among ten children and two adults—and that was a Sunday treat! Somehow, we were happy with that. We thought we were doing pretty good.

Another thing about Mama and Papa is that they had high expectations of us. They expected as much from the girls as the boys. Remember how Papa encouraged us to take Greek and Latin along with the boys?

I've been thinking a lot lately about Mama and Papa. Ever since you left us, Bessie, it seems like Mama and Papa are on my mind day and night.

I was wondering where they got some of their ideas from. I guess it was from their college days at Saint Augustine's back in the 1880s. Mama and Papa always looked up to the people they met at Saint Aug's, like Dr. Anna J. Cooper. It makes me sad that most folks today don't know who Dr. Cooper was. There was a time when she was nationally famous for her work as an educator. She pushed for educational opportunities for Negro girls at a time when no one cared about that.

I just remembered something that brings a big smile to my face. I know someone who never forgot Dr. Cooper all these years. As a matter of fact, someone's been quietly sending money to make sure Dr. Cooper's grave, down in Raleigh, has been kept up real nice, and even paid for a special plaque to remind the world of Dr. Cooper's contributions.

That anonymous person was you, little sister.

You always did live up to what Mama and Papa expected of us. You always worried that you didn't, but there's some proof.

I don't think parents have the same expectations of children that were placed on us. We worked so hard, helping Mama and Papa. We helped raise all our younger brothers and sisters. We had to do well in school and do our best; there was no other option.

Someone asked me the other day if it was all work and no play when we were growing up. Did we ever go on vacations? Did we ever go on special outings?

"Well," I told 'em, "there really was no such thing as a vacation. Folks went to see their kinfolk when they could, but you didn't go off to the beach or the mountains the way folks do today."

Bessie, they looked at me like I was crazy! They were horrified!

Then I told 'em how once a year everyone would drop what they were doing all over Wake County when the word got out that the circus was coming.

"What was it like? How many elephants were there? How many clowns?" That was what they wanted to know.

I said, "Why, there was one elephant."

They thought that was funny. "One elephant? That's all?"

I tried to explain that it was an awfully big deal at the time, but they just didn't understand.

I said, "Look. We didn't have TV, and we only knew what an elephant looked like from books. It was very exotic!"

It made me feel lonely for you, Bessie. I remember distinctly how exciting it was, and I know you never forgot either.

I remember how some of our homefolks would visit us in New York City, back in the '20s, and they would try to act nonchalant. They were country folks but they were hiding the fact that they were in awe about the tall buildings and the fancy stores.

You were so impressed with the subway, Bessie, and wanted to show it off. And those kinfolk from down South, why, they tried to pretend they weren't impressed. You came home and you were so annoyed.

You said, "Sadie, our homefolks acted like they'd been riding on a subway their *whole lives*." I laughed and I said, "Well, Bessie, they're country people and they're afraid that people will laugh at them."

And you said, "Well, I'm a country person, too, but I'm not afraid of what other people think."

Yes, that was my sister Bessie. Proud, forthright—a tribute to your parents and your upbringing. That's something I really admired about you Bessie: you never forgot where you came from.

Impatiens

"Once spring came, Bessie was
outdoors all the time. I could hardly get her
to come inside even to eat her dinner. She watched
after her flowers like a mama cat looks after
her kittens. She used impatiens to
brighten up damp and shady places.
No patch of earth went untended
in Bessie's garden."

⋘o⋙

Nine

BESSIE, YOU REALLY ENJOYED THE SIMPLE THINGS in life, like baking a cake or working in the garden or just watching the sun rise every morning. And how you loved animals: birds, cats, dogs, even those naughty raccoons who would steal from your garden.

Some folks go through life and never notice anything. They're too busy, or too self-absorbed. Not you, Bessie! That was true, right up 'til the end.

As you got weaker, you spent more time in bed, even during the daytime. But then one day, a few days before you left us, all of a sudden you decided that you wanted to be outdoors.

"Sadie, I want to feel the sun on my face," you told me. And you were so insistent. So we went out to our porch, overlooking your garden, and you sat in a chair for a while, wrapped up in a blanket although it was a warm day in September.

The next day you said, "Sadie, I want to go to the water. I want to smell the sea."

I couldn't imagine what had gotten into you. But I said, "Well, all right Bessie, if you think you're up to it." One of our friends drove us to Long Island Sound. We rolled down the car window and you looked out at the water and smelled the sea air. You said, "Listen to the gulls." I could see that you were taking it all in. It was the last time I saw you smile—you know, that big smile where you crinkle your eyes.

You always did love the seashore. When you were teaching school in Georgia—wasn't it back in 1911, or was it 1912?—you used to tell us about going for long walks at the beach and watching the sea turtles come ashore to nest.

And I remember how you used to go on Sunday outings with your boyfriend, Dean, on Long Island. That was back in the '20s and '30s, when Long Island was still like the country. You'd go to Sag Harbor and enjoy the sea breeze.

And the horseraces. Maybe that was a little naughty, betting on the horses. But we had fun, and we never bet more than five dollars. Besides, we nearly always won!

When we got older, we still had a good time. I guess we started doing more things at home. We always entertained a lot—small dinner parties—and we kept doing that through our eighties. Then we started spending more time, just us, you in your garden and me in the kitchen.

But even past one hundred years of age, we knew how to throw a party. Remember when *Having Our Say* was published and we went out to dinner and drank champagne? Now how many people over one hundred years old have a champagne party? I think that's pretty good.

And we had another party on the day we found out that *Having Our Say* was a bestseller. You were the only one who had believed it was going to be a big hit, and at the party you said, "Ha-ha. I told you so."

You never could resist saying "I told you so."

And we went to see the play about us on Broadway. Did you ever think we'd see our name in lights over Broadway? The day we went to see it the audience saw us and figured out who we were and gave us a long, standing ovation. And the actresses, bless their hearts, gave us roses.

Bessie, I'm so glad you got to do these things!

We had so much joy in our lives. Those happy days from our childhood, playing with our doll house (remember how our little sister Julia would knock all our dolls down?). Those lovely days, so many of them throughout our lives, when nothing exceptional happened, but we passed the day pleasantly.

Of course, we worked hard, too. *Hard!*

Think of all the folks you helped during your lifetime. If you put 'em in a line, it would circle ten times around New York City, I am sure.

I'm so grateful for each and every day of your life, Bessie. You used your time well.

Delphinium

"Bessie had tall stalks of delphiniums,
which were difficult to grow, and everyone
admired them. She was a very experienced
gardener, and very dedicated. It didn't
matter if a particular flower was hard
to grow; if Bessie loved it
she would keep at it."

∽o∾

Ten

It's been months since you left us, Bessie, and I see some things more clearly now.

Now I know that I made the right decision when I didn't call an ambulance or a doctor when you were slipping away. I felt ambivalent before, perhaps a little guilty. But you knew you were dying and you kept stating your wishes, and I'm awfully glad I listened.

"Sadie," you kept saying, "I want to die *here,* in my bed."

Thank you, little sister, for making your wishes so clear to me. You wanted to go when the Lord was ready to take you—not be kept alive by some manmade foolishness in a hospital.

You can never really prepare for something like this, in part because I guess you don't want to believe it is happening and in part because it never happens the way you think it is going to happen.

The end was really quite peaceful. (Thank the Lord!) You'd had a restless night and I lay awake listening to you breathe. At dawn, I heard you take a couple of deep, deep breaths in your sleep. And that was it.

I knew what was happening. I was there when Mama died, so I knew. That was the moment when, impulsively, I felt like calling an ambulance. But I knew I had to let you go. It's what you wanted. I had to do what my little sister wanted, even though it about killed me.

Had you gone to the hospital, it would have been even worse for you than most people. Truth is, Bessie, you were a very bad patient. That time you fell and broke your hip in '94 proved that once and for all. You were as naughty as you could be.

You said, "I'd rather go to the cemetery than the hospital! I ain't going to no hospital!"

I said, "Well, what are you going to do, lay here on the floor until you die?" I had someone call an ambulance. You were so mad at me, but that's what I did.

But that was only the beginning. Once they had you in the hospital, you were as bad as you could be. I had someone drive me over to the hospital so I could look you eyeball to eyeball and see if I could talk some sense into you.

I said, "Bessie, what is all this foolishness about?"

You said, "Sadie, I'm going to be as mean as I can—that way they'll leave me alone, maybe even send me home sooner."

"Well, that's the silliest thing I ever heard in my life," I said. "You must cooperate; that way you will get better sooner and you can come on home. Now stop this nonsense right now. These folks are trying to help you."

"Oh, no they ain't!" you said.

I was so mad with you, Bessie. Especially when you threatened that nice young doctor.

Well, with that whole mess behind us I knew that there was no way my little sister could possibly have a peaceful send-off at a hospital. No, indeed. I was going to have to resist the temptation to call an ambulance when the time came.

You would never have forgiven me otherwise. Why, I expect you'd have been rattling my blinds at night, raisin' Cain!

I don't think anyone wants to die the way a lot of old folks end up dyin' in the hospital these days. All those tubes. It's not natural. It's not right. And all the suffering. I'm so glad you went the old-fashioned way, little sister.

It's not like when we were children and folks died at home. Of course, plenty of times folks suffered then, too. But at least you knew no one was intentionally dragging out the inevitable. They've made dying a lot harder these days.

I hope when my time comes that my heart just stops beating. Just like that. Maybe in my sleep. I would like to be brave about it, but I suppose I'll be just as scared as the next person, that is, if I'm aware of what's happening.

I'd like to think I'd be dignified about it, if that's possible. I've lived all my life with my head held high. I wouldn't want to exit on a low note.

And they don't have to make a big fuss about my leaving. As long as someone takes me down to Raleigh and puts me in the ground between you and Mama, that's fine by me.

Pansy

"Everyone loves pansies,
especially children. They were very
popular in the Victorian era when
Bessie and I were
little girls."

∞o∞

BESSIE, SOMETHING JUST OCCURRED TO ME. IF I live just a few more years—to the year 2000—I will have lived in three different centuries!

Well, if I'm going to make it to the year 2000 I figure I had better increase my stamina. So I've been climbing the stairs at least once a day, even if I don't need to. And when I'm lonely and I can't sleep, I'll do an extra set of my yoga exercises, even if it's in the middle of the night.

I heard a funny joke. You'd have loved it. It goes like this: a one-hundred-year-old lady was asked how she was feeling and she said, "Pretty good, but you never know what tomorrow's going to bring. I ain't buying green bananas anymore, if you know what I mean."

I thought that joke was mighty funny.

I don't know what it says about me, though, 'cause I'm still buying green bananas! I guess that makes me an optimist.

I've been thinking lately that there might be some reasons for me to keep living. For one thing, the presidential election is coming up. I figure I better stick around so I can vote.

There's an awful lot to worry about in this world, isn't there? There's a lot of sorrow, but there's a lot of happiness, too.

One thing about you, Bessie—you were a world-class worrier. Now me, I figure there's some things worth worrying about and some things that's not. My philosophy always was, *If you can't do a thing about it, put it in the Lord's hands and forget it.*

Remember when we first moved into this house, how we were concerned about that big old gasoline tank we could see in the distance? And our brother Lucius said, "Don't even waste one second worrying about that."

Well, I thought he was going to say that it wasn't a danger to us. But then he said, "'Cause if it blows, you'll never even know what hit you!"

I've been thinking that a lot of life is like that. You can worry yourself to death about something awful happening, and it's a big waste of time. Probably, the thing you worry about will never happen. And if it does? Well, like that big old gasoline tank, if the nasty thing blew up, I wouldn't have time to turn and run anyway. Funny thing is, that big old tank is still sitting there. I imagine it'll outlast me.

Bessie, the one thing I really used to worry about was you leaving me first. I never wanted to go through it. I really thought it would just kill me. I've been thinking lately, *Maybe I'm stronger than I thought I was.*

One thing I've begun to see is that I had become very self-sufficient in the past few years. I'm the one who was paying the bills, writing letters, and getting the taxes ready for the accountant. Things like that.

I know you didn't want to do that kind of stuff anymore. I guess you were just plain worn out. You'd say, "Sadie, you do it, would you? I just don't feel like it." It kind of annoyed me because I had to do everything, but you had this philosophy that since you'd lived past a hundred, you didn't have to do anything you didn't want to.

Oh, you were a naughty old gal! But so very special. I know that, in the Lord's eyes, everyone is special. But I think you were really, *truly* special. I just know you got into Heaven. I know you were worried that you weren't going to get in because you could be kind of mean sometimes, but I'm sure you got past Saint Peter!

Mama always said it wasn't your fault you were a little mean. It ran on her side of the family. You were born with it! "Feisty," Mama always called it. But to tell you the truth, I always admired you for it. I always wished I could be more like you.

I always avoided confrontation. Sometimes I think that's a smart way to be. It's certainly easier. If there's a bear standing in the middle of the path, it's better to walk around him than to try to push him out of the way. Now me, I'd walk around him, most definitely. But Bessie, you'd have looked him in the eye and said, "Get out of my way, bear!"

See, I think that's crazy. But on the other hand, I partly admire it. It's an amazing thing, that kind of fearlessness.

You stood up against adversity no matter the cost, Bessie. I don't think there are too many people like that in this world. It took that kind of strength to accomplish the things you did. No one knew what to make of a woman dentist—a colored woman dentist—back in the '20s. But you were not only good, you were the best. And you helped people, whether they were rich or poor, colored or white. You didn't discriminate, although you had been discriminated against many times in your life. That takes a special kind of strength.

You never wavered in your opinions about what was important, Bessie. Integrity, faith, family—you didn't just preach these things, you lived them.

After we were discovered and we were on one of those TV shows, *The Oprah Winfrey Show*, I remember you getting mad at some of the other guests. We were supposed to be having a discussion about the important things in life, and after listening to these other folks for a while you got impatient with them and said, "I'll tell you what's wrong with people. All I've heard here today is *me, me, me.*"

It was true. Everyone there was so self-absorbed. And at the very end of the show one man even said that the most important thing in life is *money*. He just went on and on. And you wanted to give him a piece of your mind. You said to the technician, "Can we get back on? I want to set that man straight! Money ain't nothin'! He's a fool!" But the show was ending, and you didn't get your chance. Maybe it was just as well!

But you had a sweet side, too. A lot of folks never saw it, but it was there. You were gentle and respectful with those you loved. You loved children and people who were hurting. *Compassionate.* Yes, that's the word. You were concerned about other people and their feelings.

I was just thinking about something that happened on one of our very last days together. I remember checking out the house before going to bed, the way I always do—making sure the gas stove is off, the door is locked, and the faucet's not dripping. And you were so frail and thin and I didn't want to accept it then, but you were dying. You were *dying.* Yet you said, "Sadie, do you want me to come with you? Do you need my help?"

I said, "No, Bessie, I can do it myself." And by the time I came back you were already in a deep sleep. Poor little thing. You know, old gal, you never let me down.

Phlox

*"Bessie used to say that there's
nothing like a garden when it comes to bringing
folks together. White folks in our neighborhood
who we otherwise might not have gotten
to know would come by and admire Bessie's
garden. I remember one lady who
came by on a hot day and just pitched
right in, helping Bessie
water the phlox."*

Part Three

Summer came, and the seasonal progression of the blooms in Bessie's garden mirrored Sadie's own recovery. It, too, was on its own now. There were no hands but God's to tend it. Winter's sorrow had turned into spring's hope. And summer's light healed.

The same strong rays of sun that caused the flowerbeds in Bessie's garden to flourish began to nurture Sadie's spirit.

It had always been Bessie's garden. It was the one place where Bessie did as she wanted, without trying to please Sadie or do as Sadie wished. The garden nourished Bessie, and in turn that nourished the sisters' hundred-year relationship. It also nourished their relationship with their Creator.

Love, Sadie decided, must be nurtured like a garden. After all, what makes a human heart capable of love? Don't we just tend what God has given us the capacity to feel?

Even without Bessie's presence, the garden remained a focal point of life. Visitors spoke of the flowers as they came and went. A few made efforts to water the blooms or pluck errant weeds.

The garden remained a topic of conversation, a shared experience. Some flowers, like people, were having a very good year. Others were not. Much was said about what Bessie would have done, or thought, or said about a particular plant's prospects for that year. The garden caused Bessie's name to be brought up in conversation easily and frequently at a time when some found it hard to say her name aloud.

Every garden, in every climate, has its own peculiarities, its own rhythm. Bessie's flowers continued to bloom in predictable succession, conveying a sense of order that proved a comfort to Sadie. How calming to know that the tulips, or the roses, or the daylilies were likely next.

But Bessie's absence loomed large over the garden. No one could tend it as well as she. No gardener could be found who lived up to Bessie's level of devotion.

Perhaps Sadie did not wish to find a replacement. In doing so, would she be replacing Bessie?

If the garden were altered, would she be losing another piece of Bessie?

Finally, Sadie chose not to tend it. "Let it grow wild," she said one day. "Let it return to its natural state."

And so it remained Bessie's garden.

> *Do not reject me* now I am old,
> nor *desert me now my strength is failing.*

PSALM 71:9, JB

Twelve

BESSIE, I HAVE TO TELL YOU SOMETHING FUNNY. A friend of ours had been dreaming about you every night. She said you spoke to her in her dreams. One day, she was very disturbed because she had not dreamt of you the night before. All day long, she felt empty; she could not feel your spiritual presence. Fortunately, the very next day, the dream returned.

Now, here's the funny part. Our friend said it occurred to her that the one day she didn't feel your presence was the day of the Million Man March in Washington, D.C. And she said she laughed 'til she about fell on the floor 'cause she realized, "Of course Bessie's not with me today. That old gal's gone on down to see the Million Man March!"

And I laughed, because I'm sure she was right. Bessie, you were such a nosy old gal that I'm sure your spirit was in Washington that day to see what all the fuss was about. You always were quite an activist. Besides, you wouldn't have wanted to miss an opportunity to see *a million men.* No, indeed!

Right up until the end, you were eyeing the gentlemen. I remember how we had Bill Cosby up to the house just two months before you left us, and the two of you carried on like I couldn't believe. He put his hand on your knee and I thought for sure you would push it off but you didn't! His wife, Camille, who is one of the producers of our play, was there, too, and I said, "Mrs. Cosby, you'd better keep an eye on your husband 'cause I think my sister is about to run off with him!"

Oh, you were a good-looking gal and you had lots of beaux. You could have married any man you wanted but you put your career first. Little sister, you were ahead of your time!

Oh Lord, did you ever work hard for that degree. They made it so hard on you, because in their hearts they didn't want you to succeed. And I was so proud of you—imagine, being the second

Negro woman dentist in New York. Sometimes I wonder how you did it; I wonder how anyone could have done it.

I still keep your diploma from Columbia University on your dresser. I know it was one of your greatest treasures. And I put your picture next to it so that it's the last thing I see at night and the first thing I see when I wake up.

Some folks have suggested that I put these things away, but why should I? They think I'll get over you faster if I put your things away. Well, that's silly 'cause truth is, no matter what I do I'll never get over you. How can you get over someone you've lived with for more than a hundred years? And why should you try? I don't want to get over you. I just want to find a way to live without you.

Remember how, after dinner, we used to sit at the dining room table and talk? I surely do miss that! You had *good* sense. You were smart and decisive, and I relied on your judgment. Now, after dinner, I just read and pray until it's time to fall asleep.

You could look a person in the eye and look right through 'em. You knew who was honest and there were no second chances. If you didn't like someone, well, *too bad!*

Sometimes your directness was embarrassing, though. Bessie, you always did have a daring side. A few months before you left us, when Hillary Clinton came up to the house, I was worried to death about what you might say.

Before she arrived, I remember I told you, "Bessie, you must be on your best behavior. This is the First Lady of the United States coming to our home today. It's no time to be naughty."

Well, I was right to worry. I don't know why you had to go and complain to Mrs. Clinton about your big sister—me!—and how mean old Sadie made you work so hard. What a thing to bring up!

"I don't see why Sadie thinks I want to work while I'm resting," you told her. Mrs. Clinton seemed sympathetic, but she must be very wise because she didn't take sides.

And I thought I would die when you asked her—of all people!—which president she liked best. Oh, I could have killed you. But that was my Bessie, always looking to make trouble.

I remember it distinctly. I noticed all of a sudden that you had gotten very quiet and you had that mischievous look on your face—that look that always made me think, *Uh-oh*. You looked Mrs. Clinton right in the eye and said, very coyly, "So, who is your favorite president?"

She seemed taken aback but she laughed and said, "Some days it's a hard decision but most days it's Bill Clinton!"

"I'm so glad you said that," you replied. "I'd be worried about you if you hadn't!" And we all laughed.

I remember how Mrs. Clinton got up from her chair to look at our family Bible. "I don't think I've ever seen a more beautiful Bible," she said. And then we talked about the importance of education and family. She said we'd made a big contribution by showing people the possibility of living a good life, a godly life. "Washington," she said, "needs your wisdom."

It still makes me smile to think of that. At least I've got memories like these to keep me going.

Sunflower

*"Bessie used to say that nothing
represented the glorious days of summer quite
like the sunflower. She planted smaller varieties as
well as the great big towering ones, and at
the end of the season she would collect
the seeds and we would eat them."*

∞○∞

Thirteen

Our nephew Harry, the doctor, was here and he said I'm doing fine—just watch that I don't fall, things like that. You know, those old brittle bones.

Harry asked me how I was feeling and I said, "Well, I'm still kicking, but not as high." That's really how I feel. I think I'm doing pretty good for such an old lady.

I got a new summer dress as a gift from one of our kinfolk, and I look sweet in it if I do say so myself! I didn't look a day over forty, if you ask me.

You used to laugh at my vanity. Remember how I was worried I'd have a scar after I broke my hip and had surgery? You thought I was silly. You said, "Sadie, you're 103 years old. What are you worrying about some old scar for?"

Well, I didn't care how old I was, I never had no scar in my life and I didn't want to start then, no thank you. Every day, twice a day, I started rubbing vitamin E oil into the incision and, Bessie, you can hardly see it at all anymore.

Some of our friends that are twenty, thirty years younger come in here and tell me they're worried about me, but to tell you the truth, I think I look better than they do.

They come huffing and puffing up the steps and I'm thinking, *I hope you don't die in my parlor!* (Isn't that naughty?)

I miss some of the things we used to do, Bessie, like when we fixed our hair. We'd go to the big sink upstairs and wash our hair and do it nice. Never had anybody do my hair other than you and Mama in my whole life. I try to fix it myself, but it's not as good as the way you did it. It's times like that when I really miss you, notice you're gone.

It also bothers me when things happen, like somebody is born or dies, and you're not here to share it. Our cousin Al up near Hopewell Junction died, and when folks came in the door to see me I said, "Mama's cousin Al died." But I could see that it didn't mean much to them. It would've meant something to you.

I guess Al must have been in his nineties. Last time we saw him was at the family reunion three years ago. I thought he might make it to one hundred, but you didn't think so. And you were right.

Now you see, that made me feel lonely. Your passing has made it harder to be this old, Bessie. When you were here to share things, it wasn't so hard being over one hundred years old. There was someone else who remembered the same things.

Sometimes there's events in the news, like elections and things, that make me very much aware that you are not here. You would have commented on them, had an opinion. Like the deliberate burning of black churches that I heard about on the radio. We would have been grieving over that together. You'd have been ranting and raving about it!

I really felt your absence, strangely enough, when they had the Olympics in Atlanta. I listened to it on the radio and it brought back so many memories of me and Mama and Hubert at the Los Angeles Olympics back in '32. You didn't come with us because you wouldn't leave your dental practice unattended, so I sent you postcards every single day. When I came home, I told you all about it.

California was so pretty I wanted to move there, remember? But you said there was no way you were going to move somewhere where the ground moved under your feet.

I'll tell you something else I miss. I've had to deal with some practical things without your help.

The gutters on the roof need repairing and it's got me in a tizzy. Remember how we always put things like that off? We kept thinking, *We're so old, why bother wasting our time with that?*

I know you would have handled running the household alone better than I. I can cook and do all those things, but you were the one who was mechanically minded. Why, you could fix anything.

You knew how to repair the furnace, and I don't have a clue. You knew how automobiles worked, and airplanes, and all kinds of gadgets. Maybe that comes from being a dentist. That's the kind of mind you had, the mind of an engineer and a scientist.

Where did you learn these things? Must have been from watching Papa. I guess I was so busy being a Mama's child and working in the kitchen that I didn't realize how much time you spent with Papa. I remember how Papa could take that Hammond organ apart, fix it, and put it back like new.

One of your best qualities, Bessie, was the way you observed things. You studied things without saying a word. People used to say that when you looked at 'em, you were looking right through 'em.

Well, I wish I had some of your skills. I didn't realize how much I relied on you, Bessie. Now I'm learning how to make it on my own.

Rose of Sharon

"When we were little girls,
our Grandma in Virginia had a wonderful
rose of Sharon growing on her property. Many
years after Grandma died, Bessie and I visited
the old farm and found that the rose of Sharon
was still blooming. We clipped a little
sprig and Bessie planted it right
by our front steps in Mount Vernon
so that every time we'd come and
go we'd think of Grandma."

༄

Fourteen

BESSIE, THERE'S NO ONE LEFT MY AGE, NOW THAT you're gone. One by one, everyone my age has died.

I was looking at my address book. Just about everybody in it is dead! I was thinking of putting together a new address book, but I didn't like the idea of leaving all those folks' names out, even if they have gone to Glory.

One of our young friends wrote a letter for me to one of our old friends back in Raleigh. And the letter came back. It couldn't be delivered. Well, we finally got the right address and got the letter to him and he wrote and said, "I haven't used that old address since 1930!"

It reminds me of when *Having Our Say* was published and the publisher wanted to know if we knew anyone famous who might recommend the book. "Jacket quotes," I think they called it. Well, we knew lots of famous folks, like Booker T. Washington and Dr. Du Bois, but everyone was dead. I said, "If we could communicate with Heaven, we could get us some mighty fine jacket quotes."

The only one left living at that time was Cab Calloway. We knew him from our Harlem days. They contacted Cab and he wrote a real nice jacket quote, which was awful nice of him. I think he was a little surprised we were still living. But now he has died; I've outlived him, too—and he was quite a bit younger than me.

I really have only one old-time girlfriend left, our old friend Edith from Philadelphia, and she's in her nineties, I suspect.

I don't know how she did it, but Edith managed to get to the big funeral service we had at Saint John the Divine. Hired a driver to bring her all the way from Philadelphia. And just recently, she came all the way to Mount Vernon to see me, just for the day! She said it took three hours just to get here. Then she had to turn around and go back. I said, "Girl, you're crazy." But I was awful glad she came.

Edith brought me a present—a little TV with a device that lets you watch movies. *Watch movies!* I don't like TV very much and you know I haven't been to the movies in about a million years. But this means I can watch movies at home! Imagine!

My favorite is about a darling little piggy named Babe. It reminds me of the pet pig you had when we were little girls. Oh, Bessie, you would have loved this movie.

I remember how Papa didn't want us to go to the movies when we were young. The movie theaters in Raleigh were segregated and he didn't want us to face the indignity of sitting in the balcony.

Our friends and homefolks think it's funny that I like to watch movies on my new machine. Now everyone's bringing me movies. Of course, I think they're only showing me the nice ones.

All our people still come around to see me. They look at your empty chair in the parlor and your empty bed and get the saddest look on their faces. Some of our friends and homefolks are so young, I don't think they've had too much experience with dyin'. I feel like I have to help them through it. I tell 'em, "This is the way God planned it."

Young people keep your mind alive, don't they? I always want to hear what is happening in their lives. I learn a lot about the world today. In some ways things are harder for young folks today. They have more choices than we did, Bessie; they have a lot of temptation. They're under so much pressure, so young, to have sex and to do drugs.

On the other hand, they have it easier than we did. They have more opportunities than we would have dreamed of. They don't work as hard or as long, and they don't have to go through that Jim Crow mess! But they sure do love to complain. I guess every generation thinks they have it the hardest.

Some of the young folks are into separatism of the races. I say no; that's not the way. Colored and white need to mix together. That's the only way. I don't think racial prejudice will ever go away completely, but the more we work together and just *be* together, the better things will be. Folks will see we are all just human.

I feel very strongly about my opinions, Bessie, but I'm not sure I express myself as clearly or forcefully as you did. I'm learning that I have to speak up. I used to let you speak for both of us.

Now I have to say what's on my mind. Maybe I've just gotten so old that I don't care as much what people think anymore.

Some things I would have just let go I don't anymore. One of our friends got in a fuss with her neighbor. She was so angry at him she wouldn't speak to him.

She said, "I'm never going to speak to him again."

I said, "You're just going to walk past him every day, and not say a word?"

She said, "Yes, I will."

In the past, I would have said something like, "Tsk, tsk, what a shame." Instead, I got more involved, just like you would have, Bessie.

I said, "Child, you cannot let this little fuss become a big fight. You must not do that."

"So what should I do?" she asked.

"Tomorrow morning, when you see him, you must nod and say good morning."

Well, she didn't like that at all. But I kept after her until she gave in. She came to me one day and said that she finally said good morning to her troublesome neighbor. To her surprise he gave her a great big smile and all was smoothed over.

"I feel so much better," she said.

I said, "See, I told you so." And I laughed to myself afterward because I realized I sounded just like you, Bessie.

Morning Glory

"The blossoms of the morning glory
last only a day or so, but there are always more
to replace them quickly. Bessie admired
their trumpet shape and vibrant blue
color and declared that no garden
was complete without a smattering
of morning glories."

❧

Part Four

*T*he flowers of August warned of summer's demise. Somehow, to Sadie, this made them even more precious. Like the waning days of life, the last blooms of the season are not taken for granted.

Fall was coming. Flowers that had emerged from the earth, that had grown strong and tall and bloomed in all God's glory, faded and died. Sadie still held her vigil in the window, but now a shawl was curled about her shoulders to ward off the chill.

In years past, long shadows and cooler evenings were a signal that soon it would be time for Bessie to leave the garden and retreat to the house for the winter. *Yet Bessie never mourned the passing of summer,* Sadie thought. Bessie had understood the earth's need for rest. How clever God is, Bessie often said, to devise these four seasons.

Perhaps the gardener, more than other humans, accepts that everything has its moment in the sun but then must pass on. How else, Sadie wondered, could there be room for next year's flowers?

Sadie thought of nature's cycle of life, death, and returning life. She found peace and beauty in the knowledge that Bessie's flowers would be reborn next year. In Bessie's garden, Sadie had found a gentle reminder of eternity.

"Tell me, Yahweh, when my end will be,
how many days are allowed me,
show me how frail I am.
Look, you have given me an inch or two of
life,
my life-span is nothing to you:
each man that stands on earth is only a puff
of wind,
every man that walks, only a shadow,
and the wealth he amasses is only a puff of
wind—
he does not know who will take it next."

PSALM 39:4–6, JB

Fifteen

PEOPLE ASK ME HOW I'M DOING THESE DAYS, Bessie, and I say, "Pretty good, pretty good. As well as can be expected."

Things are working out as well as they could have. Of course I miss you, and I expect I always will, 'til the day I die. Looking back, it's so clear to me how fortunate you were. I made a little mental list of your blessings, Bessie—

A life well lived, full of love and joy and hard work and giving.
A life ended on a high note, with recognition for your spiritedness and good deeds.
A life so long and prosperous 'til the end.
A peaceful passing to the Spirit World, with little suffering.

How happy I am for you, Bessie, that you had all of these things. It surely makes it easier to let you go.

What is harder to understand is when young folks die, or folks in their prime. Remember how we felt when our little nephew, Little Hubie, died so long ago. Ten years old, and sick every day of his life. Cerebral palsy; I think that's what they call it today.

And our brother Hap's son, Henry, who died at fourteen. He was just a boy. Went swimming and the next thing we knew he was on his deathbed with meningitis.

You were so good to both of those boys. I remember how you helped look after Little Hubie, taking him to all those special doctors. And Henry—well, you took up stamp collecting just so you and he had something in common. He'd come over to our apartment and the two of you would work on your stamps together.

If Henry didn't have time to come in, he'd knock on the window of our apartment as he walked by. And we always knew who it was.

Some folks live a long life and never really appreciate it. At least Little Hubie and young Henry knew love. They knew happiness. They were personalities, put on this Earth for some reason. They didn't leave a big mark on this world but they were here, yes indeed, and I remember them with love.

Up in Heaven, maybe Little Hubie isn't sickly anymore. Maybe he's running around in a field, laughing his sweet laugh. And maybe Henry is swimming or working on his stamp collection. Do you grow older in Heaven? Or are you the same age as when you died? I wonder.

I imagine that Henry and Little Hubie were there to greet you, Bessie. I know they were waiting for you.

Black-eyed Susan

*"Black-eyed Susans grew wild in the yard
in Mount Vernon. We found them growing there
when we moved in, and Bessie said, 'Let's keep 'em.'
Bessie considered wildflowers to be a gift
from God. It would have been a
sacrilege to remove them."*

∽o∾

Sixteen

A FRIEND OF OURS HAS STARTED SENDING ME newspaper clippings about old people, Bessie. Would you believe there were some folks in those articles who were even older than me? Why, there was one lady in Paris, France, who was 121!

I don't know how in the world anyone could live to be 121. And the newspaper said she's still got her senses and everything. They say she had a tenant who waited around for years for her to die so he could take over her apartment—but she outlived *him*. I think that's kind of funny.

Before I read those articles I was worried because I thought, *I can't possibly live much longer.* Now I'm thinking, *Hmmm, maybe I've got a few good years left in me yet!*

Old folks today are doing more than anyone ever thought they could. Why, when we were children, folks were knocking on death's door after turning fifty. Sixty was ancient, absolutely ancient. Living to one hundred was unheard of, really.

Mama was considered old when she had her first baby at the age of twenty-six! Now women are having their first babies at forty and even older.

It seems to me that if you've got your health, you can stay young a long time. I think you can keep going past that century mark as long as you're healthy and have got a reason to live.

I don't see why folks should retire at sixty-five. I retired at seventy myself and, looking back on it, I bet I could have kept teaching for a long, long while yet. Of course, they make you retire.

To think I've been collecting a pension from the New York City Board of Education since 1960. I bet they never thought they'd have to pay it this long. They'd have been better off if they'd let me keep teaching!

I loved my students. I loved being in the front of the classroom, looking at all those young faces. I knew I was making a difference in their lives. To this day, I still hear from some of my students!

Now, of course, I have my second career. I came out of retirement at 102 when we started working on *Having Our Say.* It was splendid having a job again.

I think all people over a hundred should have a job. Keeping busy is as important as having companionship.

As soon as you left us, Bessie, folks started asking me, "What are you going to do now?"

I didn't even hesitate. I said, "I'm going to get to work—on another book!"

Folks laughed when they heard that, 'cause they think it's funny that this 107-year-old lady is so ambitious. But it's not ambition that drives me. It's having a sense of purpose. A reason to get up every morning.

Another job I have, which I take very seriously, is to teach young folks. I'm trying to educate our kinfolks about the old days, about Mama and Papa and our grandparents and so on. I miss how you and I used to talk about our homefolks, so now that you're gone, I just retell our stories to the young relatives and our friends. I tell them about Jim Crow laws and all that meanness, but I tell them funny things, too, like the silly things we did when we were children. I tell them about Mama and Papa, and about our grandparents, and what Raleigh was like one hundred years ago. I tell them what it was like to come to New York during the First World War and how hard we worked. I think they'll remember us, and our stories, long after we're both gone.

One thing I'm finally able to do is talk about you, Bessie. I like to tell stories about you. For a while I couldn't talk about you but now I can. It makes me feel good. It's like having you here beside me again.

Snapdragon

"Bessie generally didn't let folks pick flowers
from her garden unless they were headed to the
cemetery. Then she'd say, 'Help yourself
to anything you want.' Snapdragons
seemed to be everyone's favorite."

∽○∾

Seventeen

Bessie, a friend of ours said something recently that meant so much to me. I had the blues and she was trying to lift my spirits.

She said, "You gave Bessie a gift. Do you know what that was?"

I asked her what she meant.

"Why Sadie," she said, "you let her go first."

You let her go first.

I had been laying on the daybed and I sat bolt upright. I thought, *what a lovely thing to say! Of course! Of course! I wouldn't have wanted it any other way!* Bessie, you never had to know what it was like to be the one left behind.

I would rather be the one doin' the suffering. I'm not enjoying it, no indeed, but I'd still rather that I went through it instead of you.

My little sister never did like the idea of being left behind! So, for once in your life, you did something first. Ahead of me.

I remember how you complained about being in my shadow. Not long before you left us, you weren't very hungry one day, and I remember the girl who was helping me cook tried to inspire you to eat.

"Come on, Bessie," she said. "You need to eat. If not for yourself, do it for Sadie."

Lord, did you get mad. "Why do I always have to please Sadie? When does Bessie get to do what Bessie wants?" Oh, you were all worked up.

I just laughed. And that made you laugh at yourself. Just think of it, two sisters both more than a hundred years old and squabbling like two little girls!

But I understand how you felt. It couldn't have been easy being the younger one. All the teachers in school expected you to be like me. And in the hospital, when you broke your hip a few months after I did.

That young doctor said to you, "Following in your sister's footsteps, eh?" Boy, did that ever make you mad.

And then that nurse said to you, "My! You're not anything like your sister."

"Why should I be?" was your answer.

I'm sure it wasn't easy being in your big sister's shadow for 104 years. You complained about it a lot but I know you'd have been miserable without me.

Well, I'm glad things have worked out the way they have, because you never had to be alone, Bessie.

Funny thing is, though, by leaving me here by myself, you're letting me get the last word. Ooooooh, I'm not sure you would have liked that!

Money Plant

"Bessie adored the money plant,
but not the real thing. She had no interest
in money or material things."

Eighteen

I'M STARTING TO GET ACCUSTOMED TO SEEING your chair empty. Remember when Mama died how every time I looked at her empty chair I'd start crying? And you thought I would never stop crying and that I would die, too?

Well, it occurs to me that I *did* get over Mama's death! And I started thinking, *If I got over Mama, maybe I can get over Bessie.*

Losing your sister after living together for more than a hundred years, well, it's a pretty terrible thing. It's like you opened the front door of your house and stepped inside, only there was no house, just a hole in the ground and you keep falling and falling.

It's the same feeling, whether you lose your Mama or your sister. And I imagine it's the same as losing a child or a husband or wife.

But what are you going to do? Lay down and die? Jump off a bridge? Somehow or another, you live through it. You keep breathing. It's out of your hands. Your body does it whether you want it to or not. Next thing you know, you've gotten through the first day, the first week, the first month.

Life is never the same. It chills you down to your bones. But I was thinking, *the Lord never promised us that this life would be easy. No, sir.* Think of our people who were slaves. I think of them and I'm ashamed at feeling sorry for myself.

Life is a vapor. That's what the Bible says. It passes in a blink of an eye. We're all so busy with the details of living that we don't always appreciate it.

I remember how I always had a list of things to do. I'd say, "Now, Bessie, we really need to do this and that."

And you'd say, "Oh, Sadie, must we?"

One time, I remember you telling one of our young folks, "I believe life was meant to be pleasant." You waved your right hand to make the point, the way you do when you really wanted to emphasize something.

I believe life was meant to be pleasant.

All right, Bessie, I'm hearing you. I'll do what I can to make life pleasant without you. I know that's what you would have wanted. You wouldn't have liked the idea of me pining away here without you.

I'm glad you used to say things like that. I'm glad I remember you saying these things. It makes me feel like I have your permission to keep on living, and try to be happy.

That was a gift you gave me, wasn't it?

. . . till you grow old I am He,
and when white hairs come, I will carry you
   still;
I have made you and I will bear the burden,
I will carry you and bring you to safety.

ISAIAH 46:4, NEB

Chrysanthemum

"Bessie always noted the passage of time
through the blooms in her garden. The budding
of the chrysanthemums signaled the arrival of fall
as surely as the crocus had announced
the onset of spring. When the
chrysanthemums bloomed,
we knew that summer
was waning."

౿౦ళ

WE ALWAYS CELEBRATED OUR BIRTHDAYS TOGETHER. I guess we started doing that way back when, because it was easier for Mama. The school year had already started by the time my birthday came around on September 19, so Mama gave us a party together on your birthday, September 3.

I remember Mama saying, "Sadie, do you mind celebrating your birthday with Bessie?" And I said, "No, Mama." And I meant it. I never minded sharing with my little sister. It's funny. I was two years older and you'd think I would have wanted my own party.

Well, we went and shared our birthday party for the next hundred years or so out of habit, I guess. But now, with you gone, I wondered if maybe I should do things differently.

Then I realized that I should keep celebrating your birthday—just as we always celebrated Papa's birthday every year! We always cooked a special meal, with all his favorite foods. Every February 5 since he died, back in '28, we had a party for him in his honor. It was a way of celebrating his life.

Well, I decided to do the same thing for you. I'm going to do things just the way you liked: a small party in the late afternoon with a few dear friends and kinfolk. Naturally, we'll serve Boston coolers and your favorite coconut cake. I'll put some flowers from your garden on the table, the way we used to.

I was just thinking about your favorite quote from the Bible:

> But they that wait upon the Lord shall renew
>   their strength;
> they shall mount up with wings as eagles;
> they shall run, and not be weary;
> and they shall walk, and not faint.

ISAIAH 40:31, KJV

I figure if I wait upon the Lord, I can get through anything. Why, I've started making dates on my calendar again. My datebook is just about filled up with visitors. I better get some rest if I'm going to do everything I want to do.

Somewhere along the line I made up my mind I'm going to live, Bessie. I guess I probably don't have that much longer on this Earth, but I may as well make the best of it. Since the Lord has given me this long life, the least I can do is be grateful. How can I give up on myself when the Lord hasn't?

Bessie, I think I'm going to be all right.

Cosmos

*"A day or two before Bessie died,
the cosmos were blooming and someone picked
some for us on their way into the house. I put them
in a vase on Mama's writing desk, which was
at the foot of Bessie's bed, so that she
could see them. Flowers always
made Bessie smile."*

∽∾

Twenty

A FUNNY THING HAPPENED, BESSIE. SOME OF our friends threw me a birthday party. They said, "Sadie, it's about time you had your own birthday party. You only turn 107 once!"

Well, you know I never had a party of my own in my whole life. It felt so very strange, but it was lovely. I didn't expect to have a very good time, but I did. I felt thoroughly spoiled. I said afterward, "I declare that this is the best birthday I ever had."

There was a surprise that you would have loved, Bessie. It was really a present to you, too. You won't believe it, but they've officially named a rose after us—the Delany Sisters Rose! A man named J. Benjamin Williams in Silver Spring, Maryland, bred a new rose in our honor.

It's two colors, red for you and ivory for me. The red is 'cause you loved red and anyway you were so feisty. And the ivory's for me 'cause you know I love that color and I'm the sweet sister. Oh, it's splendid. I thought only folks like the Queen of England got to have a rose named after them. I don't think we're important enough, but I surely do appreciate it.

I got a lot of other presents, too. I got a hand-bag—patent leather, with three zippers—and a new baseball cap. You know how I like to wear baseball caps when I read in my chair by the window. Keeps the sun out of my eyes. Oh, and I got a silk scarf and baskets and baskets of flowers.

We had a cake with seven candles. Everyone's tired of trying to fit one hundred plus candles on my cake every year. They said, "We're starting over! Like the odometer on a car! You're seven years old today!"

And I said, "Does that mean that pretty soon I'll have to be a teenager all over again?"

So now I am officially launched on my 107TH year. Never in my life did I think I would live this long. I'm getting as old as Moses.

It was in the newspapers that I had another birthday. That just tickles me. I think it's kind of funny, being famous so late in life! It has certainly made life interesting.

Now that I'm past my birthday I realized that in a few days it will be one year since you left us, Bessie. I've been on my own for a year now. I'm going to spend the day sitting in your garden and writing letters. I'm going to keep busy and look toward the future.

Remember how I used to say, "Life is short, and it's up to you to make it sweet"? Well, I was wrong about that short part. But I still believe it's up to each person to make the best of life, to keep trying, no matter what. A lot of it is how you look at it. A lot of it is attitude.

Don't worry about me, Sister Bessie. Child, I've got *plans*.

Rose

The Delany Sisters Rose.

∽o∼

On My Own at 107